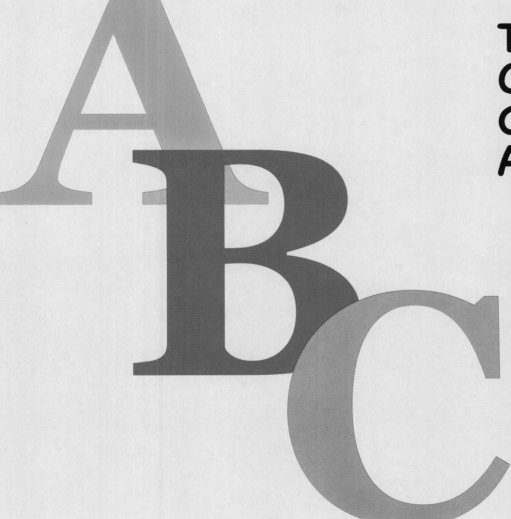

The Official Cleveland ABC Book

Elephia Press
www.elephiapress.com

The Official Cleveland ABC Book

Images and Text © 2019 Mark Zannoni
www.markzannoni.com

Published in 2019 by
Elephia Press
19885 Detroit Rd., Suite 208
Cleveland, Ohio 44116, USA

ISBN 978-1-8897-4821-4

Library of Congress Control Number: 2018912622

10 9 8 7 6 5 4 3 2 1
First Edition

Printed and bound in the United States of America

The Official Cleveland ABC Book

Images & Text by
Mark Zannoni

ELEPHIA PRESS
Cleveland

A

Airplane

Where would you like to visit?

B

Buildings

How many buildings can you name?

C

Construction

How tall can a building be?

D

Doctor

Why is it important to see the doctor?

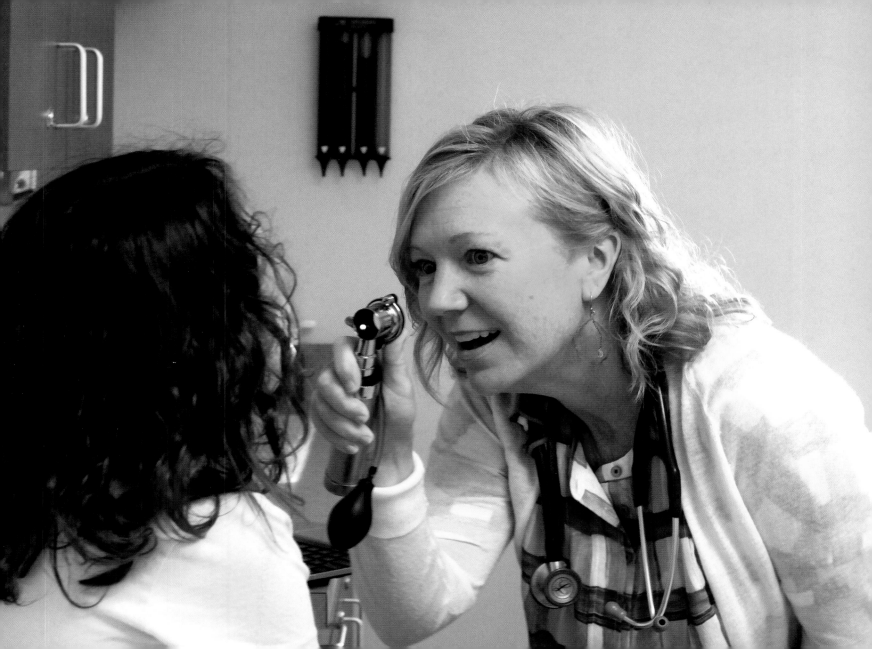

Elephant

What is the largest animal that lives on land?

Flag

What does a flag stand for?

G

Graffiti

Where have you seen graffiti?

H

Highway

What is the difference between your street and a highway?

BEGIN
SHOULDER
AUTHORIZED
BUSES
ONLY

I

Industry

What can you build in a factory?

Judge

Why are judges important?

K

Kayak

Have you ever been on a kayak?

L

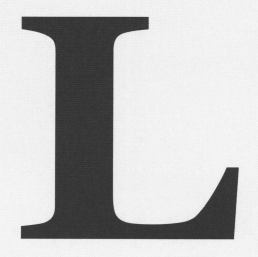

Lake

Do you know how to swim? Can you see the skyline in the distance?

M

Market

What is your favorite food?

N

Newspaper

Do you read the newspaper each morning?

Obelisk

Have you ever seen an obelisk before?

P

Port

How many ships do you see?

Quarter

What can you buy with a quarter?

R

River

How many rivers can you name?

Stadium

What is your favorite sport to play?

T

Train

Which American city had the first rail transit line connecting its airport and downtown?

U

University

What subjects would you like to study?

V

Veterinarian

What kind of doctor is a veterinarian?

W

Winter

What are your favorite things about winter?

Xylophone

What instrument would you like to play?

Y

Yield Sign

What is the difference between a yield sign and a stop sign?

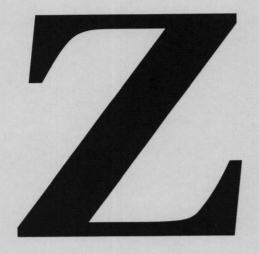

Zoo

What is your favorite animal at the zoo?

To Dante & Sophia

Acknowledgements: Thank you to those who appear in this book. Your presence contributes to its richness and grace. I am also very grateful to those who assisted in this volume's production. And finally, thank you to Dante, Sophia, and the City of Cleveland who inspired this project.   -MZ

Key to Images

Airplane - a Delta Airlines Boeing 757 on approach to Cleveland Burke Lakefront Airport (BKL)
Buildings - Cleveland skyline from Lake Erie
Construction - One University Circle on 23 July 2017 - completed in July 2018
Doctor - Brenda McGhee, MD
Elephant - at Cleveland Metroparks Zoo
Flag - Official flag of the City of Cleveland
Graffiti - at Columbus Rd. & French St. in the Flats
Highway - Shoreway near E. 55 St.
Industry - in The Flats
Judge - The Honorable Solomon Oliver, Jr.
Kayak - in the Cuyahoga River
Lake - Lake Erie at Huntington Beach
Market - West Side Market
Newspaper - *The [Cleveland] Plain Dealer*
Obelisk - at E. 79 St & Hough Ave., Hough
Port - the Port of Cleveland at dusk
Quarter - in a parking meter on Detroit Ave.
River - the Cuyahoga River
Stadium - Progressive Field
Train - a Red Line Rapid Transit train at Hopkins Airport Station; answer to the question: the first
         US city connecting its downtown and airport with rail transit service was Cleveland in 1968.
University - Case Western Reserve University
Veterinarian - John Reveley, DVM
Winter - a snowy street in Lakewood
Xylophone - a two-octave wooden xylophone
Yield Sign - at Liberty & Stokes Blvds, University Circle
Zoo - Cleveland Metroparks Zoo; the animal is a wallaby